Prelude

Prophetic patterns are part of a change in the real reality; it isn't a change in the Bible or the words God gave. It is an enhanced message to clarify what was also given. The prophetic patterns are pieces where the scriptural run into the natural. They are, specifically, what you remember with what's going on now. These pieces to the pattern are building to the end result.

You were called for this. Throughout these lessons, you will have to ask yourself where you first felt a 'shift'. You will have to realize that patterns are visible when the eyes and ears are heightened. During your time of clarity you will have to pray, fast, and pray.

You will have to answer how the patterns change the mainstream. Is it through wisdom or through release?—what do you hear in the release?

TESTIMONIES:

My testimony from the first teaching was that it had been said to me to make myself busy while going through my trials.....on the call it was reiterated to do mundane task while waiting to hear from God!!! I had also been told to relax my mind and my brain. After the call the next day I was watching TV which I rarely do and the Lord spoke loud and clear to me.

I can't wait until the next class....so excited for what God is doing in this class and in our lives. Dana is awesome and I am so grateful for her!!

Erikka S.

This was a strange start to this teaching.{Part I} I've invested in something that I knew would be different, but not so different, that I'm questioning every little thing in my life. I won't quit because if this is TRULY GOD AS YOU SAID, I have something to learn so that I can help! Thank you.

Anonymous

TABLE OF
CONTENTS

ISBN-10: 0988229366
ISBN-13: 978-0-9882293-6-5

The advice and strategies
contained herein may not be
suitable for your situation.

For more information about Dana
Neal and Coach Dana Enterprises
Visit   www.coachdana.biz,
www.baduniversity.com   or
Contact the business office at
414-301-1236

www.baduniversity.com

PART I
THE CALLING

Looking at all the
pieces to the pattern

**John 7:17King James Version
(KJV)**
*17 If any man will do his will,
he shall know of the doctrine,
whether it be of God, or whether
I speak of myself.*

CHAPTER ONE: HOW THIS ALL STARTED

God teaches us and takes us through various tasks, and lessons, for what is necessary for our servant-hood in the kingdom.

There is nothing in life, that doesn't **TEACH** us for the next levels of life, we will be on, and all that we will go through.

God gave me more end time revelation in the three months He 'trained me', that I never would have seen, had I not been obedient, and realized how peculiar I was as a prophet and seer.

This is how Prophetic Patterns came about.

Walking in various levels of the prophetic, each of them is heightened for what is necessary for me to see and act on at any particular moment.

Everything that God gives should be acted on in one way or another; they are the pieces to the pattern. The way God taught me this lesson, may seem like a mundane task to others, but necessary. Our minds work wonders doing mundane tasks. God will use whatever and whomever to get His point across and to train us in the particular gifting HE has given.

There are prophets that were sent before me that may not have known they were prophets. There are prophets among us that don't understand what they are seeing or even doing. Some things that people have seen in their lives, they could have assumed it was déjà vu, but that is the world's definition of a prophetic occurrence.

There are seers that were sent before me that may not have known they were seers; they could have assumed it was just a dream or a trick of the eyes.

God will reveal the necessary pieces to the pattern in His way. Some different ways, which I'll pinpoint in this teaching, are in television shows or songs.

CHAPTER TWO: WHAT IS A PATTERN?

In order to answer what is a pattern, we must first know the meaning of a PATTERN

The regular or repeated design or way in which something happens or is done (www.merriam-webster.com)

Patterns for various objects are different. Consider the architectural design of buildings, or patterns for clothing. Patterns are the puzzle pieces put together to form something uncommon or unique.

Prophetic pieces to the pattern don't come in a box. They are an enhanced message to clarify what was already given at different points in our lives.

Some things are vindictive of a pattern or a shift. The reason why you picked up this teaching is because you know you are different. It may cost you your sanity if you try to fight against it.

The patterns in your life don't always add up. The pieces you can't explain are, right now, beyond you. Why? These patterns are what you remember from your past, with what is going on now. With these pieces you will be able to see more you're your spiritual eyes, and provide more understanding.

My personal pieces look like this:

- My name being called 3 times in my life
- I didn't realize it was the Lord until the year 2010 or 2011
- Called to ministry
- Déjà vu, as a child actually being the prophetic anointing

on my life
- Having the Seer Anointing
- Apostolic Mantle
- The Lord speaking directly to me in dreams and visions
- My hearing heightened
- Instructions increased

These pieces are what God does in our lives that we can't tamper with. Or change. Our own understanding, wants, and needs, can't trump God's plan; each pieces creates the pattern of HIS purpose.

We can make the decision to follow the devil, but when we decide to follow God, the pieces of the puzzle, of those strange unexplainable things, start to form a pattern and come together in a visual that couldn't be seen, while walking with the devil. *In some cases, it could be seen, but not understood.*

PERSONAL REFLECTION:

_____

_____

_____

_____

_____

_____

_____

_____

_____

_____

_____

_____

_____

_____

_____

_____

_____

_____

CHAPTER 3: WHO SEES THE PIECES TO THE PATTERN?

First let's answer this question that I know is in the back of your minds: Yes, there are false prophets. We know they will come and what they will say; they may even try to confuse us.

Now, who sees or saw the pieces to the pattern? The person who saw the pieces to the pattern is the one who isn't even aware they still see it. They are trying to apply it to their current, or let us say common life. How do we know? Well let's go back to some of our previous examples and add more to the list:

- Science fiction novels
- Television shows

- Random conversations w/unlikely people
- Confirmation of what God has shown YOU through an unlikely person, place or thing

There are people around you that see exactly what is happening, and what is going on between the natural and spiritual realms. These are either prophets sent by God or the false prophets that went.

The problem in understanding what is given to them, and even you, is how they respond to the pieces and reveal the message to others.

Some of these people could be prophets that are sent, but left the narrow path in order to obtain their worldly desires. Some of these desires include control; controlling someone is witchcraft.

How do we know?

Things that you have seen out of the corner of your eye, or that you feel are unexplainable, but are explainable when the spirituality is heightened.

Is it important?

It is vital to your understanding and the future of the entire world. How do you confirm it? By studying to show yourself approved; read your Bible.

CHAPTER 4: WHY AREN'T THE PIECES MORE CLEAR?

The pieces to the pattern are revealed in a way necessary for a particular time. The clarity on the pieces is visible to those that can truly see and hear. You will have to leave the logical you behind in order to see the pieces clearly.

The pieces reveal how the natural and spiritual realms truly intertwine. They align with the Bible from Genesis to Jude, which means you must read Revelation is the finished puzzle The book of revelation doesn't touch on what has happened in all the books It is prophecy for what is about to come.

What have you been given in your life where the book of Revelations confirms that? All the 66 books have taught you something.

Nothing I am sharing takes away from the word of God, and being Holy in your living. Those that see the pieces that form the pattern will be around to help you as co-laborers in the gospel.

PERSONAL
REFLECTION

_____

_____

_____

_____

_____

_____

_____

_____

_____

_____

_____

CHAPTER 5:
WHAT WILL YOU DO FOR THE ONES YOU LOVE?

Throughout these lessons, you will have to answer the questions on the following pages; you will have to discover whom you really are in, and with God, to go on.

The pieces to the pattern are significant for each person. As you are a father, mother, husband, wife or ministry leader, you will have to say that you can't go to hell on a technicality for the sake of your position in LIFE, but your POSITION IN THE AFTERLIFE.

In all honesty, you will have to decide to let go, and truly let God. You have to know that you have shared the gospel and the truth will prevail. The pieces to the pattern of this puzzle of your life will come together in your obedience.

Are you a parent? What will you do for your child? Are you a ministry leader? What will you do in the calling God has given you? Are you employed with the government? What will you do that will go against your job description? Are you teenager? What will you do that your clique doesn't?

Look at your life as whole; as a parent each child you have has a different attitude, and spiritual make. Look at your job description; your spiritual man shouldn't change just because you're at work. Look at where you live; you shouldn't be afraid of your surroundings because God has His angels over you.

Look at where you fellowship; you may have to move on because they can't see you've moved up. God calls, chooses, trains, and qualifies.

CHAPTER 6: BE READY FOR DISTRACTIONS

Every message isn't for you. Learn not to attend every conference (business or spiritual). Learn not to stand in every prophetic line. Every person isn't for you; you may have to walk away from some people. Even family; you may have to decide not to be so social.

Every time you get closer there will be a distraction. The enemy will use any and everything to throw you off course; circumstances, people, and even money. Every time you get distracted, there will be a way out. What is that way out? Reading your BIBLE consistently.

Distractions come to test you and detour you. How you respond to the distraction will help your elevation which is discussed in Part II. If you allow the distraction to keep you DISTRACTED, you can get off track.

Are you armored up for that battle? These distractions could be a death, or a birth in your family, a loss in income, being homeless, or health issues. Distractions harm you when you aren't reading your word and being consistent in your studies.

CHAPTER 7: BEING ESTABLISHED

Establish meaning: is to cause (someone or something) to be widely known and accepted to put (someone or something) in a position, role, etc., that will last for a long time to begin or create (something that is meant to last for a long time)

You are being established for that next level. Everything you have seen or have been through is pushing you forward.

Where will God take you? You will have to fast, and pray more than you have recently. You might have to get away from all people for a short time.

The spiritual realm is real!! God will show you things in the spiritual that no one can handle in the natural because you are being established!

The road to take is narrow. Every one can't go, so the road will only fit the team and only few will understand. The people that are being prepared to go with you will understand the call and the journey.

Establishing you will change you. Whatever religious doctrine you have been taught will not match up with what is coming next. The training from the Holy Spirit is very different than the training from man/flesh. That is why you won't find BAPTIST, CATHOLIC, COGIC, etc, in the BIBLE.

The pieces, so far, will start to make sense; every strange thing will start creating that PATTERN!

1 Peter 5:10New King James Version (NKJV) *10 But may the God of all grace, who called us to His eternal glory by Christ Jesus, after you have suffered a while, perfect, establish, strengthen, and settle you.*

PERSONAL
REFLECTION

_____

_____

_____

_____

_____

_____

_____

_____

_____

_____

_____

_____

INTERVAL

This is the point of no turning back. Some of you may not be ready for this, and that's okay, but a decision has been made if you've come this far.
You can sit back and ponder the idea, or you can move forward continuing to put the pieces to the pattern together.

In each lesson, you will personally discover something that will shock you, and might scare you, but as someone once told me, will you be scared enough to keep moving or no?
You have 4 more parts to finish, and apply.

PART II:
NEW LEVELS

Pieces are being formed into the pattern

CHAPTER 1: WHAT ARE PROPHETIC PATTERNS?

Similar to a puzzle, patterns overlap and connect for the end result. Whatever the destiny, it becomes a pattern by recognizing what happened initially in dreams and visions. The world calls it DÉJÀ VU when it's actually a prophetic occurrence; a pattern. When you start to put all the pieces together, you get the message, hence, forming the pattern.

What was the message given to you? God said something that caused you to pause in whatever you were doing at that particular time that you recognized the call. The message is part of the pattern.

The prophetic gift was revealed. Do you recall when God first called you? Did you hear the voice? Did your pastor/leader? What did you do when you heard it? I know we talked about this in the first part, but reminding you about it helps you to keep it fresh in your mind.

Were you at all afraid? Did you journal it? Where is it written? These patterns cannot be explained by the human concept, because they are always spiritual. These patterns are inferences from God that we cannot change. They are part of life that we brush off or don't second guess; strange or weird, so we don't think about it. Prophetic patterns are part of the abnormalities in life that can be explained by spiritual relationship with God. This includes discernment. You will have to determine if you are an anomaly which we'll talk about later.

Once you eliminate the impossible, whatever remains, no matter how improbable, must be the truth. Author Conan Doyle, Brainy Quotes

John 16:13 King James
Version (KJV)
*13 Howbeit when he, the
Spirit of truth, is come,
he will guide you into all
truth: for he shall not
speak of himself; but
whatsoever he shall hear,
that shall he speak: and
he will shew you things
to come.*

Strange patterns bring you to the
truth. You will find that you see
things that aren't there. You will find
that in your waking moments, you
hear some things going on in the
spiritual. Go back to part one and
consider the way God will reveal the
pieces and to whom.

Look at what is happening round the
world:
- The Ebola breakout in the U.S.
- The murders in every state

- Cop killing unarmed suspects
- Kidnapped girls in other countries
- Children against parents

Of human action and reaction everyone looks to the government or law enforcement, but who has prayed? Have you prayed? Who has studied history? Someone knew this would happen long before it did.

CHAPTER 2:
QUESTIONS WILL
ARISE

What would you do as a husband/father? The head of the house will need to make tough decisions, what will those decisions be? Will he be emotion driven? What would you do as a wife/mother? She will have to decide to use her knowledge and not her heart. She will have to decide to use her heart and not her worldly knowledge.

What would you do for someone you love?

- Friends
- Family
- Team Members

What would you do as a teacher or ministry leader? What you think you know may not be what is actual in your life.

So, what would you change? What you desire to change may not be what is needed. Would you put your goals ahead of the safety of the people? The people matter more than your bottom line. If, you know your foundation, your bottom line will **help** the people.

These are questions, because there will come a time where you will be struggling to stay within the normal realm of things and not know what to do; what to chance. The normal realm isn't where you want to be, because as a peculiar people we aren't normal! You will have to be willing to take a chance when it isn't LOGICAL to take a chance.

As a true prophet and servant of God you will have to think out the logical box. Will you be willing to sound stupid or strange? What are you willing to chance to change the outcome? Losing a child maybe? Consider Job; he lost everything. Would you be alright if you lost a spouse? ...a Career?

You will question your very sanity as a person Everything will seem like its coming from a scary movie You will frantically seek answers from those that can't help you In the 3 months God trained me, I asked various prophets to interpret my dreams. One prophet NEVER ANSWERD me; others, were off point; I had to hear from the Holy Spirit personally! Some visions and dreams prepare for end time Things that haven't happened yet Things that show you in a place or time that hasn't come. The importance of keeping track will bring up more questions Journal EVERYTHING!

PERSONAL REFLECTION:

_____
_____
_____
_____
_____
_____
_____
_____
_____
_____
_____

CHAPTER 3:
PECULIAR PEOPLE:

1 Peter 2:9 King James Version (KJV)

9 But ye are a chosen generation, a royal priesthood, an holy nation, a peculiar people; that ye should shew forth the praises of him who hath called you out of darkness into his marvellous light;

This scripture takes us into trying to understand an Anomaly. What is it? Why/How are we an Anomaly? We are, as saints, a peculiar people. New levels will bring enhanced prophetic occurrences; dreams and visions won't be like what you've had before. What you hear will not be able to be explained. *On September 2, 2014 my hearing intensified and has been heightened ever since.*

Who DON'T you want to be? There will be a time that you will see you and not want to become that person. God will even give you visions of who you might become if you don't change now. What is your perception? How you see others, from the outside, is how you will react. Go back to chapter 1 of this part, and look at human action and reaction. This is why understanding an anomaly is so important. Anomalies are strange to people and can be explained by definition, extremists theories, and religious rhetoric, but the truth is, every peculiar person is a 'spiritual anomaly' (if I may say) that can only be explained by the definition of a prophet in the Word of God: THE BIBLE.

CHAPTER 4:
AN ANOMALY

What is an anomaly?

> Someone or something that is abnormal or incongruous or does not fit in. That deviates from what is standard, normal, or expected.

Why is it? It isn't exactly a why but truly a how. The why is its necessary, the how depends on the gifting and when it was received. Are you an Anomaly? Yes.

Whatever gifts you carry for KINGDOM building cause you to be peculiar and abnormal! Saints are a peculiar people.

God is the head of our lives. There is

no changing that, but understanding the pieces to the puzzle that create the pattern is where you have to know WHO GOD IS AND WHY HE CHOSE YOU.

You will never understand the purpose, but you will know it is a purpose, and how you respond to it. This is how you are different and you are peculiar.

Ask yourself about anomalies from an unknown perspective. Look at everything around you that has happened; the planes crashing, diseases, & deaths. The state of the religious state of mind; what do I mean? People push the doctrine and not the Holiness.

What are the ministry leaders accepting? There is homosexuality in the church; there are Pedophiles in the church. How can I say this? Look at the different people places or things in the Bible that happened because God spoke it. We can explain the spiritual because it's in the BIBLE.

Reminder: An anomaly is someone or something

How did you meet or network with the people you are connected to?

- Social networks
- Church
- Other friends

Would they be in your circle under normal circumstances? What about the things you do in your life? Do you watch certain TV shows, or not at all? Do you listen to certain music or not at all? Read certain books or not at all? Can you explain what you see and hear? People won't trust you; are you ready to lose friends?

PERSONAL REFLECTION:

_____

_____

_____

_____

_____

_____

_____

_____

_____

_____

CHAPTER 5:
TEAM

Clarifying an anomaly will show you that each facet of your life including the people, places and things develop a team. The team is given to you by your obedience to the factors that have molded you into who you are now, and whom you will become. You won't even know some of these team members personally.

Each member of the team is part of the plan, or in this case the pattern. Each one has a specific gift, or talent, to help you accomplish the goal. Compare this to the 5-Fold Ministry; Apostle, Prophet, Evangelist, Teacher, Pastor.

People received prophesy that they were part of my team, but they never fulfilled that position. The enemy came in as a distraction. He will use friends and family to detour any of us. Personal circumstances will come in to play, but placing the pieces to form the pattern still has to be done. You will still have a job to do. Obedience is better than sacrifice.

CHAPTER 6: ESTABLISH THE FOUNDATION

When going to new levels there is a price to pay.

> Luke 12:48 King James Version (KJV) *48 But he that knew not, and did commit things worthy of stripes, shall be beaten with few stripes. For unto whomsoever much is given, of him shall be much required: and to whom men have committed much, of him they will ask the more.*

How much more time will you put in to study? You will have to read, and re-read the word of God. God's word is pure: Proverbs 30:5 *Every word of God is pure: he is a shield unto them that put their trust in him.*

This is nothing **MORE TRUE TO THE I'S DOTTED AND T'S CROSSED** than the word of GOD. The Lord speaks to all that want to hear and do. What holds you still, but keeps you alive? The word of God does. The Lord is still preparing you in that still place.

There are people who really see the future and they aren't psychics. There are people around you, smarter or more advanced than you, spiritually, that will not share what they know until absolutely necessary. For your own protection you're on a need to know basis. Are you ready to look ignorant and do what is necessary? People won't believe you nor will they trust you.

This is End time. Are you ready to die

for being a Christian? Are you ready to be deceived by the enemy while you're being prepared and even pruned?

Look again at what is going on around you: the RFI chip. Is that the mark of the beast? No matter how cute it seems. What about legalized Marijuana? What happens when your addictions become your living nightmare? Addictions are strongholds that you need deliverance and release from. Be ready to win. For the kingdom!

You will see past your limitations. Armored up! Walking upright! Obedience is essential and key to growth. God is watching no matter what.

Faith trumps all! Believing in what you don't see will help open your spiritual eyes and ears. In faith you can do the work, the assignment, given to you.

Forgiveness is also essential; it is needed to see your assignment clearly! You must forgive and forget. Not forgetting is the ball and chain that hinders true forgiveness. People that depend on their emotions will forget that forgiveness is essential.

CHAPTER 7:
FAITH BASED
INVESTIGATIONS:
FBI

You are, and will become an FBI agent. Faith Based Investigator. Some personal secrets, will never want to be revealed. Even secrets about yourself will come out and it will either push you forward or will set you back; all depends on how you respond to the closet's open door.

You will not want to do what is expected of you. The thought of giving up is natural, but you have to press on! Your piece of the pattern will cause you to die to flesh, and live in the spirit from now on.

What's hiding in you? There are some things that you know that you aren't aware you know, that are about to be pulled out. Searching for what is right on the edge of your imagination is being an FBI Agent.

Some information given to you will be necessary for later. Some people will give up what they know because what they know is scary, and they don't want to be responsible for keeping it in! Will you be ready to accept things about people you thought you knew well, but didn't? Take for instance, family: realizing your family can't help or that they don't have the relationship with God they need in order to help. They won't help even though they do have the relationship, but don't want to see you go further, or accomplish more than them. The people that love you really love you and will help.

Some people won't be able to even hear you, as you are speaking directly to them; friends, blood family, and church family. Many people know what is going on, but are literally dying to keep it a secret or hidden. Consider the man who hid his talent out of fear; fear is a spirit we're not supposed to have.

Will you die in the flesh? Or, let the flesh die? Putting the plan to work is far beyond establishing the foundations.

You are the one to investigate. It's time to ask for and obtain the wisdom Faith Based Investigator. So, to what lengths will you go? Do you have enough fear in God to move past your circumstances?

What are your abilities? You're a spiritual weapon using what you have to get what you need. Prayer and fasting will be necessary. Civilian Consultants will be the team members that God will add you to you; the co-laborers! Homeland Security, sort of speak, will be the prophets, the seers that really see and don't waver.

What exactly is Homeland?...the Kingdom of God. Studying the book of Revelations is going to be essential to understand all that the Lord is saying; focus on Revelation 21 and 22

PERSONAL REFLECTION:

_____

_____

_____

_____

_____

_____

_____

_____

_____

_____

_____

_____

_____

PART III:

CHANGES

The challenge of putting the pieces of the pattern together, and truly understanding the prophetic

CHAPTER 1:
THE REALITIES OF
CHANGE

In all honesty, wolves in sheep's clothing are mad about change. They don't want to train someone in their calling because they are fully in fear of losing them.

A war is coming. WE are currently on the battlefield, the cusp of a major, spiritual war. Everything happening in the world around us is the preparation for WAR! This war can't be won because the enemy was already defeated on Calvary. The Lord said ARMOR UP, He didn't say fight.

Even though you don't understand the change that is happening, you do not have to follow the devil. Take a deep breath to accept the change on these levels. Your gifts have been activated. Your talents are increasing.

In these changes, flesh cannot lead! People have to realize that they are no longer human beings, but spiritual beings. The flesh has to die or it will try to lead. The end result that all saints should be striving for is Heaven.

What is buried in you? You are a prophet, and most likely, a seer. You have been given the visual of the future, the past, and the present; tap into that right now. No time to walk in fear; God didn't give us a spirit of fear.

You don't have to choose to follow the devil. I know that, in life, it's easy to follow the devil, but the choice is yours. You need to stay close to God; fasting and praying is essential to staying close to Him.

You can't have the natural without knowing the spiritual exists. The things you see can be explained by what you don't see. That means all of the study you are doing in the Bible and all of the fasting and praying, will help you to explain the strange things!

Change happens when a shift happens. This is a change in the spiritual that is felt in that natural. Consider Quantum theory (IF, we have to show the science of it all) It leads to physical phenomena, which then leads to Quantum Entanglement. We'll speak more of this later, but it was very important to slip this in here. Why? You need to know that ALL THINGS, however scientific, can be explained spiritually! This is when reality gets real from the spiritual connotations that connect it to the natural.

Helping families means changing children most times. There are some adults that don't want change, but need it! Change and endurance gets too hard, so people 'seek' death. This type of death is not death in the body, but death of the spirit. They decide it's too hard, and too strange, to stay on this road. Sometimes it is the result of some tragedy that causes one to get weak. Another reason for an adult not accepting change is they can't see the ends to the means; tired of trying to be faithful. BUT, as seers, we have to recognize what we see and just be patient!

Spiritual change means learning from our current position in life and our cultural mistakes. No one wants to admit that there are some mistakes being made, or have been made, in history, in our lives; racial and gender disparities, etc.

CHAPTER 2: DOUBLE PP'S: POSSIBILITIES & PROBABILITIES

Possibilities and probabilities of life that merge the natural with the spiritual letting you know what everything is spiritual.

What have you seen, in your everyday life that you probably missed? The two worlds collide. You can't have the natural without knowing the spiritual exists. The world's laws can't help you see the spiritual ramifications. Although God didn't give you a spirit of fear, there should be that FEAR OF GOD, that if you don't be honest with yourself and know that the two worlds collide, you will be lost when the change HITS

YOU!

Studying the word of God is essential to seeing the spiritual ramifications as well as hearing from the prophets that GOD SENDS.

How you respond to the possibilities and probabilities, changes the outcome. The possibilities of what you're sharing will scare some people. They won't believe you because its too illogical to believe not only what they don't understand but also what they can't see. They will need some cosigning from others to believe what you said, but there won't be any; it will have to come from the spirit within, but that should be THE HOLY SPIRIT.

The flip side of the scare issue is that someone knows just enough about your spiritually to know that you'll make it in the call on your life, and that you're telling the truth.

Let's use an analogy to define the spiritual possibilities and probabilities more clearly: in the bathroom, you go to cleanse some or all parts of your body. Whether it be the inside or the outside, your teeth or you hair, you are cleansing the dirt out of something. This is change that happens in the spiritual as well as the natural.

CHAPTER 3:
DIFFERENCES

These differences will be discussed in more detail in Part 4, but we want to introduce them here, because you need to know not to be afraid of the detail that will be revealed.

Consider the Book of Revelation. You know that Jesus is coming back; you know that the seven churches represent something and/or someone; you know that the true children of God will be raptured up. At this point, you have to decide, with the little information you have, how you will respond to the differences and the change.

Different ideas will be placed in your head through dreams and visions; through things you read or watch on television. Different situations will arise that will need your immediate attention; things with your children, your spouse, and even your health. Different situations, or people from your past, will start to show up; people you used to date, a lifestyle you used to lead (i.e. Homosexulaity, et)

CHAPTER 4:
PAST, PRESENT &
FUTURE

You want to remember the past to learn from the future. You can't change the past but you can apply what you learned then to your present to prepare for the future God has shown you. As a prophet, when you know to share the message with someone else, you will have knowledge on how to help with what was revealed.

When did you realize you had the prophetic gifting? What do you remember seeing that you probably missed? What is coming to mind right now? Re-focus. Go back. Study your notes, and take more notes. Ask, Seek, Knock Sharing with others your gift of prophecy as directed by the Lord!

NO matter what level you are on now, no matter what piece or pattern has been revealed through now, something will come up again.

Choices you'll make to get answers will either catapult you or stump you in your learning. Not everything that you'll see or that God shows you will be able to be logically explained. You will have to decide to sit alone to hear from the Lord. You will have to decide to study and fast IMMENSELY to learn from the Holy Spirit.

Remember that the word of God is pure. God gives us a way out in His word. He knows He'll give you a chance to get it right. Are you aware that you are fearfully and wonderfully made to get that chance?

The past, present, and future overlap one another when you look at what you've seen in time We talked about re-focusing Prophets see it all as it is given to them from God God put prophets on earth to help others see what they can't explain How important is time? Better yet, TIMING? Someone is looking for you to provide the answers In accepting the change you within you, you have to see you as God sees you Capable

INTERVAL

This is where you know that you have died or need to die. This is where you know that the flesh is no longer leading you, and that you must WALK through the open door. God has opened the windows in your life, and you are looking to the other side.

Revelation 3:8New King James Version (NKJV)

8 "I know your works. See, I have set before you an open door, and no one can shut it; for you have a little strength, have kept My word, and have not denied My name.

PERSONAL REFLECTIONS

_____

_____

_____

_____

_____

_____

_____

_____

_____

_____

_____

_____

_____

PART IV:

SEEING THROUGH TO THE OTHER SIDE

The strange patterns start to fall into place, and provide revelation to the prophetic visions.

CHAPTER 1: BRINGING UP THE DIFFERENCES

In Chapter 3 of Part III, we briefly talked about differences. Let me tell you this has to be in depth in this part because this is important: differences in family; differences in health differences in life-style; differences in social response.

A difference in family and social responses is where you'll find that you don't want to walk in those circles any more. You'll find that the strange things that can't be explained to every body will keep you from hanging with every body. The enemy will use people from your past to take your off focus off your purpose.

That old lifestyle doesn't fit in this

new you. You will have to love and leave; move in your purpose while still loving unconditionally.

A difference in health is where you will show others that your faith has exceeded what people say. You will be the one that trumps the 'GOD GIVES US WISDOM, TOO' scripture, which I can't find. When you find that you don't agree with everything the doctor says proclaiming every disease, cancer, ache and pain, and issues over your body you see the world won't stand with you.

When you find that you don't agree with what the world says about what you should or shouldn't eat or what you drink you will find that the world won't stand with you. You're different.

CHAPTER 2: EXPLAINING A THEORY

We are going to tip-toe into physics (or sorts), where we'll touch on a few points in explaining Quantum Theory.

In order to explain the theory, we have to remind ourselves that natural and spiritual collide 24/7. Every millisecond of our lives runs into the spirit realm, we just brush it off. At some point you can't keep brushing it off.

There is no easy way to pick this apart without doing extensive research that God doesn't intend. So with that, here is the break down.

The below list is what happens when the probabilities out weigh the scientifically logical facts. You can study Einstein, and each term in greater detail at your convenience: Quantum Integral leads to Quantum theory which leads to Physical Phenomena which leads to Quantum Entanglement

Bringing up the PROBABILITIES again forces us to look at the definition and the why:

A number expressing the likelihood of the occurrence of a given event, especially a fraction expressing how many times the event will happen in a given number of tests or experiments. (thefreedictionary.com)

The probability of something spiritually happening is far more likely or NOT, depending on the response we give the situation.

Using "Quantum", and its derivatives, to explain the theory takes us to faith and relationship.

The relationship you have with God, and the gift of prophecy that He has given you allows you to see, feel, hear things in a certain way shape or form, that is very different from the norm.

Here, the theory, from the world's point of view, is that the prophetic isn't really real in this day and time, but if they had to TRY to explain it, we all would be seen as religious fanatics or extremists.

God will say if the equation causes more harm than good He will take it away. There is no use in bringing too much of the world's knowledge into the end result of the spiritual.

At this point, would you even care what they think, or more of what you need to do? That is where your faith kicks in.

CHAPTER 3:
THE VISUAL

Through various dreams and visions you experience the visual.

How do you share if you don't understand what you have seen or how do you explain what you don't understand?

Someone is going to look at you crazy with what you've shared. It could be that you get excited and crazy all at once. The way you detail what you have seen, you don't even believe you.

What do you shared? Do you tell it all? Everyone has to be directed by God on how to reveal what they have seen whether in a dream or a vision. Do you give them specifics or do not? Some things people will not be ready to hear. Remember Joseph and what he told his family. The understood his dream more than he, and hated him for it. You can share what you have seen when you are directed by God only.

Things you see on the local and national news were prophesied along ago. Someone was given this revelation long ago. You'll find somewhere in history that everything you see on the news, now, was prophesied. Someone was considered an extremist or fanatic; unexplainable diseases, people dying everywhere, cultural crimes, and the law against the people, travel stopped or limited.

You have to realize your vision is more intense and heightened than the rest; stories told by others. Trying to understand what others see, dream, feel you will have to take everything with a spiritual grain of salt.

Books you've read in years past have a hint of the future. Those fiction books that you enjoyed but dismissed carried some of the similarities of 'real' life.

Unexplainable things you've seen in the past are coming to 'fruition', sort of speak, now. Some examples you need to ask yourself are:

- Why in the world is Ebola here after so many years in another country?
- Colder than normal winters in all climates
  - Strange changes in weather
- Extinction events that are desperately being explained by science
  - Five major events
  - Numerous minor events

CHAPTER 4:
THE AUDIO

As the prophetic in you is heightened so will your hearing. What exactly do you hear that really isn't there? Voices and conversations by people that aren't in the same room as you are. There will be conversations that you are not in the presence of at the time, but involve you; you hear it. Things that go bump in the night or creaks in the hallway or, in the attic; some things are not your house 'settling'.

I heard God call me one cool night in the spring; this was the 2nd or 3rd time I literally heard my name; whispers in the wind. There will be songs in your spirit. I wake up from time to time with certain songs, but only certain verses of the song in my spirit; Worldly or not. What have you heard and tried to dismiss it? These songs have meaning, or they wouldn't be there.

What about door bells ringing? There is meaning to hearing the front or back door bells; front is the Lord calling; back is the past reminding you of something, or trying to get your attention.

Knocks on the door, and no one is there. Trains, Planes, and automobiles; you may hear a plane landing and shouldn't. What is coming in your life or someone's life that needs to be deciphered? A train going down your block and you're miles from the track. God is calling someone home; may not be you or someone you know but someone on your block.

What/Whom is your spirit in tune to? People will say you're crazy. Are you ready to be the odd ball?

CHAPTER 5:
NO NEED TO COUNT

Numbers are essential to understanding the spiritual. To accept this and not the demonic numerology, you have to do some serious study. Step out of the natural box and into the spiritual depths that God showed you in the visions and dreams. Understand that God used numbers in a specific way for a specific reason.

Every number given to you is pertinent; whether single digits or pairs. Every way/shape/form a number is given it is pertinent; dates, times, and money.

Just a general example, the numbers 1-10 has a basic meaning

- 1-Unity
- 2-Covenant
- 3-Trinity; Father, Son, Holy Ghost
- 4-Creation
- 5-Grace
- 6-Man
- 7-Complete
- 8-New beginnings
- 9-Fruite of the spirit
- 10-Responsibility

Find other number meanings at Asis numbers and their meanings: http://asis.com or anything by Bonnie Gaunt

CHAPTER 6:
NOT ACCEPTED

In this part you will have determined that your acceptance in your purpose will cause you to be an outcast. Are you ready to be alone? Although they see you alone, God is with you. Remember you have to see yourself as God sees you and that is capable.

God will send you help. Those that understand and see you from a distance will help you get through.

Remember you are a peculiar person. With this view, from both sides, there is 1. no turning back and 2. no trying to fit in. Refer back to the new wine in old wineskins and how it won't work.

You have been given a glimpse into the other side and no one will understand that. Even after this teaching, there will be some things you will have to force yourself to accept. Right now is the time to see the greatness, and be ready to armor up completely with the knowledge you already had, but are now activating.

CHAPTER 7:
THE JOY OF THE LORD IS YOUR STRENGTH

The enemy will try to take your joy. He knows you know He doesn't want you to stay on the Lord's side. He truly doesn't want you to know that you are capable to fulfill your purpose.

What do you have to fight with? You have the word of God. It is what you take on the battle field. Ask for wisdom. Another piece of the puzzle is being aware that your mouth, mind, and prayer time will keep you in GOD'S face asking for wisdom to keep moving. With that wisdom do you know what you have to stay armored up? Fasting and prayer!

PART V:
DOORS

The various pieces to the pattern are your personal keys, and spiritual options to destiny.

CHAPTER 1:
THE DOOR IS OPEN

In the book of Revelation the Lord talks about the open door Revelation 3:8King James Version (KJV) *8 I know thy works: behold, I have set before thee an open door, and no man can shut it: for thou hast a little strength, and hast kept my word, and hast not denied my name.* You are ready to walk through; no more questions to be asked. Just obedience in doing what you are told to do. The door signifies the opportunities that were given and you accepted them without hesitation.

The open door signifies that you have what you need to walk through. There is nothing wrong with you. No more issues with being peculiar or being an anomaly. The open door is approval. The open door is another level in the spiritual; you have seen the other side, now your gifts are activated at a point where you cannot turn back. Many things will need to be accomplished

CHAPTER 2:
THE KEYS ARE IN
YOUR HAND

There is no need to look for common keys There is no need to look for any more understanding in using the keys **The keys are the word of God The keys are the pieces that were placed on the inside of you as you went through your calling The keys are the pieces to the pattern that you will need in walking through this door They are the notes you took throughout your growth process** Don't look for anyone to approve the keys

CHAPTER 3:
IN THIS WORLD, BUT NOT OF IT

You will have to go back to the old neighborhood. You will have to share the gospel despite what is going in their lives. You will have to cross the same streets you crossed before, but with the word of God. You will have to go the same routes with a different attitude. You will have to allow the same friends to see the new you. Carry your Bible and prepare the way.

Never let go of the keys you were given to use as you walk through those open doors.

This world will have to take you as you are NOW, and accept it or run from it. You can't worry what they think or you'll lose focus. You can't forget those that are with you for the sake of those that are against you. The new you has to be so BRIGHT they don't want to be against you, but want that same GOD IN YOU. Stay on course because the war is at hand End-time, Rapture, The Apocalypse.

If you start worrying about the people, the doors may be lost to you even though still open. God can/will close the doors as well.

Chapter 4:
LEFT BEHIND OR NOT

Your prophetic gifting can see the now or the later. Consider the prophet Isaiah. Now that you know what you have seen or heard in the spirit is real, you have to help those decide not to be left behind. John had to write the book of Revelation as it was given to him not changing a word. Those that will be left behind, have a choice to make, and you'll have to share that too.

INTERVAL

One thing, I think saints forget is that we have to understand someone will be left behind; those that we think should have been part of the 'first group'. They may not be the first to get raptured up, but they still have a choice. We have to say RIGHT NOW, if you are left behind, you have a chance.

Chapter 4 cont.

What risks will you take? The closer we get to Jesus coming back there will be many chances you will have to take that will risk your life on this side. The one risk you can't take is taking the mark of the beast. You will have to make sure you follow everything God shows you. What battles in this war will you choose to be a part of? Remember God said armor up, not fight, but to armor. Remember you won't be alone, even though you will be seen alone.

CHAPTER 5:
I LOVE YOU

In earlier parts of this lesson, we talked about what a parent, spouse, friend would do. Decisions will need to be made regarding those close to you. Each and everyday, no matter how clear things get in your prophetic walk it will be hard to focus on the purpose. The love can't be lost. You can't stop loving anyone the way God loves you, but you still have to stay on task. The choices made mean what? They mean God trusted you with the keys to use in the open door, not to open the door, but INSIDE THE DOOR!

You will have to let go of those people, places and things that you have tried to hold on to. Loving and living, you have the time to love on your family, friends and others.

No matter the purpose, make sure you love and show love. Time is of the essence. God gives you time to do what is necessary, especially in the purpose of kingdom building.

Day and night; month after month you have to love and live. Days will start to turn into nights, and months run into years. It isn't age, its time.

CHAPTER 6: ACCEPTANCE ON ALL SIDES

Previously we talked about the things you see happening in the world and the glimpses from the spiritual realm. These will be things you have to accept; sicknesses, death, etc. Romans 1:18King James Version (KJV) *18 For the wrath of God is revealed from heaven against all ungodliness and unrighteousness of men, who hold the truth in unrighteousness;*

You can NOT be in a place not to accept what is happening on both sides. The issues in the world that they accept are trumped by what God said. What you see in the spiritual are warnings or instructions!

Nothing will be as it seems. Everything will seem to get worse before it gets better. Remember how you respond will be more important than the issue at hand. More things will be unexplainable.

Everything in its right place; no matter how good or bad it seems. Pieces to the pattern will become clearer. The power you have to heal, deliver etc will be heightened. Sharing the word of God and living holy is essential. People will want to live Holy and follow the Lord.

CHAPTER 7:

THE END IS NEAR BUT NOT HERE

This is the end of a 5 part series and the last chapter in this part. This has been a tough journey, but it doesn't end here. Prophetic Patterns is the piece that makes it all clear.

The irony is that until the rapture happens, I have to give this teaching. God took me through three months of training, so that I could teach this lesson that others haven't taught; not because they don't know, but that they are afraid of what people will think.

The enemy has been on a rampage. I have had issues trying to get this done from start to finish; distractions, family issues, finances etc, but I didn't stop.

No one knows the day or time The day nor the time has been told but here we are in the midst of the chaos that is the fork in the road that PROVES THE END IS NEAR Matthew 24:36 *36"But of that day and hour no know, not even the angels of heaven, but My Father only"*

- Preparation is key
- Praying
- Fasting
- Continuous studying
- Ministering in the streets

You will come across people that have been waiting on you; those that know there is only a remnant and you're part of that remnant. will be positioned to help you keep going They will be very conscious of the keys that you have in your grasp. You will come across people that want to stop you; they too are well aware of the keys and will try to take them from you. They will try to prostitute your gift which will cause you to lose focus. You can't afford, spiritually, to lose focus.

Be mindful of the end result. Be mindful of the people watching you. Be mindful of the decisions you make that will affect your destiny. Be mindful that you have to stay on this journey until God calls you home. Be mindful that you want to be part of the first.

START YOUR MINISTRY

With all of the pieces you have been given, there is still more work to do. We discussed continuous studying of the word of God; THE BIBLE. With all the keys that you have established in these pages, you have to continue on this journey that you decided not to run from.

Start your ministry; fulfill your purpose; do your job for the kingdom.

Bless you!

ABOUT THE
AUTHOR

Dana Neal was born and raised in Milwaukee, WI. She is a wife, mother, and CEO (Christian Encouragement Officer)for many business and organizations. Dana Marie started writing in elementary and high school where she wrote short stories in her spare time and poetry for her schoolmates.

Accepting her calling as Pastor and business woman, Mrs. Neal works as a business and lifestyle coach, helping her clients see that spirituality and business go hand and hand. You can always hear her say never run your ministry as a business, but business can be used as ministry; a testimonial for others!

Bless you as you go forth in all that God has for you!
Dana Neal
www.coachdana.biz
www.baduniversity.com
414-301-1236